The Organizational Role of Supervisors

Jack Asgar, Ph.D.
based on original work by

Frank Hoffman

Practical Management, Inc.

First Edition

9 8 7 6 5 4 3 2 1

Library of Congress Catalog Card Number: 89-61070

ISBN 0-9622797-0-6

Copyright © 1989 by Practical Management, Inc.

All rights reserved under International and Pan-American Copyright Conventions. No part of this book may be reproduced in any form or by any means, electronic or mechanical, including photocopying, without permission in writing from the publisher. All inquiries should be addressed to:

Practical Management, Inc.,
P.O. Box 8789, Calabasas, CA 91372-8789
(818) 348-9101

Contents

Preface	v
Introduction	vii
Chapter One	1
What Supervision is . . . Who? And Why?	
Exercises	10
Chapter Two	25
The Supervisor as Head-of-Workgroup	
Exercises	31
Chapter Three	39
Coordinator with Other Supervisors	
Exercises	49
Chapter Four	59
Supervisor as a Member-of-Management	
Exercises	70

Preface

This book is based on the original work done by Frank Hoffman, co-founder of Practical Management, Inc. (PMI). His work was presented in audio cassette/workbook format as complete self-instructional material that included various case problems and exercises. In this book, we have tried to separate the exercises from the body of information. The reader, however, is encouraged to complete the exercises for full application of the concepts. This book, as was the previous work, is for people who are now supervisors. Managers should read this book, not for themselves, but to learn how they can be instrumental in developing their subordinate supervisors.

Introduction

The role of a supervisor, as differentiated from that of a manager, often is very hazy in a multi-level organization.

In some cases, every level of management gets involved in supervision and duplicates the supervisor's function. Often these misuses of functions are justified on the basis of "Management by Walking Around," "Show of Interest and Concern with the Worker," etc. These management fads and euphemisms not only produce negative results, they will cause other deep-rooted problems for the organization.

First, by management levels doing the job of the supervisor, managers do not have time to perform their own managerial duties which are essential and distinctly different.

Second, when an organization recognizes that managerial activities are not being performed, the organization creates additional levels of management--causing the burden of unreasonable overhead costs.

Third, the managers usurp the function of supervisors, not allowing the supervisors to learn and strengthen themselves. No amount of supervisory training is going to compensate for the lack of opportunity to perform.

Fourth, at best these misuses of functions are going to create many duplications of effort.

Organizations have to realize that supervision is different from managing and that each level requires a different set of skills and a different set of responsibilities. Various levels of the organization are not the result of outgrowth from the previous one. We truly do have levels of discontinuity in organizations. For example, when a worker gets promoted to supervisor, he or she must realize that this new position is different--not only in superficial issues such as title, salary, benefits, perks, parking locations, etc., but also in the nature of the work. Supervision requires learning and performing supervisory skills.

Also, when supervisors become managers they have to recognize that level of discontinuity. Managers are not glorified supervisors. Their function is substantially different, and they too have to learn and perform these different functions. One of the important realizations is to "let the supervisor supervise." This simple statement is the essence of success. Those who do not understand or practice that simple axiom are doomed to reap the poor results of their own doing.

The preliminary conclusion of the study conducted by Columbia University (Human Resources and Practices in American Firms, by John Thomas Delaney, David Lewin and Casey Ichniowski) indicates that a significant issue in determining a successful organization depends on strengthening the authority of the first-line supervisors and expanding their control.

The purpose of this book is twofold: (1) to delineate the unique functions of the first-line supervisors and to guide them in how they can function effectively in the "real world" and (2) to inform managers on what performance they should expect from their subordinate supervisors and to guide them in achieving productive results from their workgroup.

Jack Asgar– *Los Angeles, California, January 1989*

CHAPTER

What Supervision is....Who? And Why?

At first it might seem these questions are too simple to ask: "Who is a supervisor?" and "Why do we have supervisors?." It might be obvious that supervisors are those people in an organization who have subordinates working for them, and that we have supervisors to make sure that work is done as effectively as possible. However, as we begin to define the job of a supervisor, it becomes clear that the job is much more significant than just having others working for a supervisor, especially when we start considering a supervisor on the management team. When we look at any sizable organization, we can identify seven distinctively different positions:

1. "Mission Workers": The non-supervisory people who perform the work of the workgroup, headed by a supervisor. For example, the mission of an accounting unit is to perform the various accounting requirements of the organization.

Therefore, those who actually do the job of accounting (accountants, accounting clerks, etc.) are "mission workers."

2. "Personal Service Workers": The non-supervisory people who work directly for a manager or a supervisor. They provide the manager or supervisor with advice, help, or service, but do not do "the work." Secretaries and staff assistants are good examples of "personal service workers." (It is important to know that "mission workers" and "personal service workers" are two separate kinds of positions, because only one of these qualify the boss as a supervisor, as we will indicate later.)

3. "Lead Workers": The people who have some supervisory responsibility but whose mission work assigned load is so heavy that there is really little time for true supervision.

4. "Supervisors": The people who have mission workers or lead workers reporting to them. This position is extremely important because they are charged with a unique responsibility which is not asked of other members of the management team.

5. "Managers": The people who have supervisors or other managers reporting directly to them. There may be two or more levels of management in larger organizations.

6. "Top Executives": Members of top management who have managers or supervisors reporting to them, plan the organization's future, figure how to acquire necessary resources, and establish overall policy.

7. "Staff Specialists": Those who serve line managers with specialized advice, but who have no mission workers, supervisors, or managers reporting directly to them.

Having a personal service worker (such as a secretary) reporting to a person does not qualify that person as a supervisor. Only mission workers and lead workers reporting to an individual will qualify that person as a supervisor. Also, titles do not qualify a person as a supervisor or manager. Titles are often given without any consideration to the organizational role of that person. Defining a true role of a person by the title does not allow the organization to develop a true "team-player."

When you realize a supervisor is a person who has mission workers and lead workers reporting directly to him/her, then it becomes apparent that:

1. The supervisor needs first-hand, day-to-day knowledge about the specific methods and techniques by which mission workers should be doing their work.

2. No amount of knowledge and skills in human relations, communications, leadership, planning, and organizing can compensate for a lack of familiarity with job methods and techniques. This important supervisory requirement is so vital that without it we have no true supervisor. We may have a boss, but not a supervisor.

Everyone agrees that a supervisor must also prevent errors before they happen, not only after they happen. After an error has been made, everyone can recognize the error. Everyone can tell if an account doesn't balance, an engine doesn't start, a plan is not complete, but only a supervisor with job knowledge can recognize the error while the mission worker is working on that accounting, making that engine, or drawing up that plan.

The supervisor exists to be that member of the management team who has expert knowledge and understanding of the specific methods and techniques by which mission workers should be doing their work.

This means that supervisors do not do the same kind of work as managers. The supervisor exists so that the work gets out. Managers should be concerned with resource management and planning for tomorrow so the work can get out. The supervisor is concerned with getting the work out today. The manager's concern is to provide the resources (anticipating the needs for tomorrow's work).

When these two positions (managerial and supervisory) get confused, the organization does not perform as a team.

If a manager is involved on a day-to-day basis with the methods and techniques of mission work, that manager is performing a supervisory role no matter what the title he/she uses. How would you like to be on a football team with two quarterbacks calling the plays simultaneously?

The supervisor plays the most significant role as a member-of-management. Therefore a full-fledged supervisor has to fulfill three major responsibilities:

1. As a head of a work group
2. As a coordinator with other supervisors.
3. As a person representing management to mission workers, and mission workers to management (being a member-of-management).

Head of a Workgroup

The primary task of a supervisor as a head of a workgroup is to make sure that the work gets out, error free, meeting quality standards, and according to budgeted cost. In order to accomplish this major accountability, a supervisor needs to be involved in technical details of how the work is going, how it should be going, what the equipment is capable of, and whether workers are doing the work in a way that will meet quality, cost, and schedule requirements. This will reduce or eliminate the problem of facing unsatisfactory products or services after the fact.

Some organizations provide a supervisory training program which teaches that supervisors should "manage," that is, not get involved in day-to-day operating details, but spend their time doing forward planning, setting overall goals for the workgroup, and reviewing progress at periodic intervals rather than as the work is going on.

If these teachings are implemented by a supervisor, the unit will face:

--Work errors found afterwards.

--Late deliveries and unmet schedules.

--Possible problems with other interrelated work units.

--Complaints from other supervisors.

--Finding out problems after higher management questions the issues.

--Spending time and effort doing "detective" work to find out what happened.

--Mission workers not receiving needed help and assistance.

--Lack of necessary know-how by mission workers when they are faced with different or difficult tasks.

--Lack of immediate knowledge when the supervisor is asked by the boss about a particular piece of on-going work.

If the supervisor's job becomes "managing" (so that both manager and supervisor are focused on plans and goals, overall schedule targets and standards, etc., but neither is in daily contact with the on-going work), then no one is supervising. The certain result of this is unproductive work.

Supervision must happen if the work is to get out properly, but if supervision is not done by supervisors, managers will not manage, they will supervise.

Involvement by the supervisor in the on-going work does not mean looking over the shoulders of mission workers constantly, but to check with mission workers on how they are coming along against the schedule (are they having problems with the in-coming work, etc.).

Coordination with Other Supervisors

It is the job of a supervisor to make sure that the organization functions as designed. This duty requires supervisors, not managers, to coordinate with other units.

Let us examine this concept. Assume we have an organization charted below:

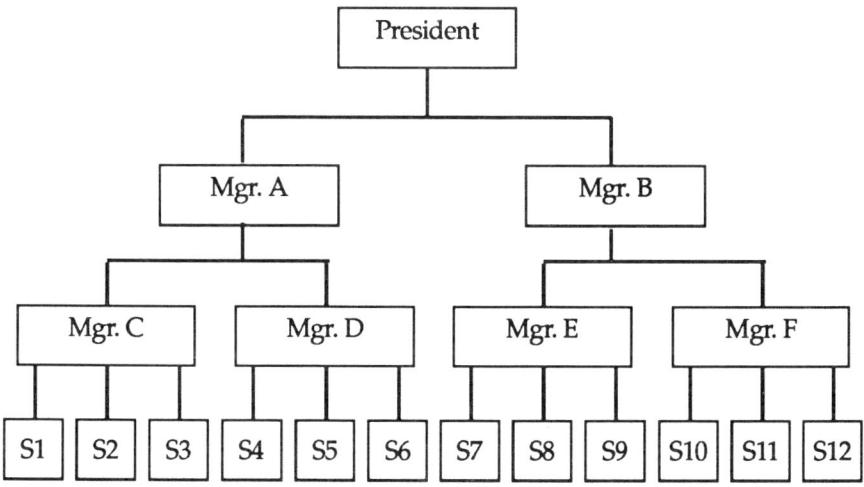

Whose job is it to coordinate unit S1 with unit S3? And whose job is it to coordinate unit S10 with unit S12?

(If you have said Manager C for the first case and Manager F for the second case, you believe that coordination is their function because they are the common boss in each case.) Now who is to coordinate work unit S1 with work unit S4?

With that reasoning you must say Manager A, since Manager A is the common boss of those two units. Then who should coordinate work unit S1 with work unit S12?

The President? (The only common boss of these units, with that reasoning, is the President.)

Would you want the President of your organization to adjudicate problems between the lowermost units of your organization or work on the future direction for your organization?

Coordination is a lateral function, not diagonal or triangular. When we talk about supervisory coordination we do not mean coordinating the mission workers job, but rather coordinating laterally with the heads of other mission work units (other supervisors). Lateral coordination by supervisors will allow the organization to work effectively as designed. Supervisors cannot be expected to have authority and control over all services and resources their workgroup must call on. However, a supervisor cannot circumvent the organization by bootlegging work, or ignore the poor cooperation of another unit on the basis that "it is not my job." A supervisor is responsible for getting the job done by getting work done through the organization using lateral coordination.

Member-of-Management

As the mission workers look upward into the organization, they should see the supervisor as a person representing management. This concept means that the supervisor must be the first management person they call on for all issues, not only methods and techniques of the job, but also clarification on benefit plans, personnel policy, etc. Also, as managers look downward, they should see the supervisor as an important link between themselves and the mission workers.

In the subsequent chapters, we will discuss the three important organizational roles of a supervisor in greater depth.

Summary

Chapter One

--Supervisors are those who have mission workers (or lead workers) reporting directly to them.

--Supervisors are identified by who reports to them, not by their titles.

--An organization's titles for supervisors, managers, and staff specialists often do not tell you who plays on the management team. Since supervisors and managers each have different kinds of people reporting to them, supervisors and managers should each do different kinds of work.

--A manager should not focus on the same goal as the supervisor. The main focus of a manager's time and attention should be on something other than "to get the work out."

--Supervisors should be more knowledgeable than managers about how workers should do their work and about how errors and accidents happen.

--A manager's reason for checking the work in progress and dealing directly with mission workers should not be to "get the work out," but to check on how well the supervisors are doing their job.

--The supervisor should have complete authority and final say over salary increases, disciplinary actions, terminations, performance reviews, official documentation to the personnel file, etc. for immediate subordinates. As a full-fledged, first-string member of the management team, there are three basic roles the supervisor is called upon to play:

1. Be a head of a workgroup.
2. Coordinate laterally with other supervisors.
3. Be a member-of-management.

--It is not the rightful role of managers to coordinate one supervisor's unit with another. That is a primary role of a supervisor.

A supervisor cannot expect to have authority and control over all the services and resources the workgroup must call on.

The supervisor is responsible for getting the job done...not by substituting for other parts of the organization, but by getting things done through the organization.

Exercises

The following exercises are designed to increase learning by application. For the best result you should read the exercise and respond to the questions asked. Then, you can compare your answers against the "correct" answers given. If the explanation given is not sufficient, review this chapter or the related segment for clarification.

Exercise One
The XYZ Company Case

Otto, Supervisor of a six-person workgroup, has had these questions and comments from his boss, the Section Manager, so far this week:

A. "I noticed an odd whirring noise in the copy machine, so I told the operator to avoid running it at top speed. When you get over 80 percent speed on that model, the belts tend to slip and squeal."

B. "The people in procurement have been complaining again that your workers aren't putting the correct charge numbers on their supply requests. So, I've given Mary, Sam, and Tillie a schedule whereby each of them will spend an hour over the next two weeks in procurement to see the problems they're causing."

C. "Yesterday when the Department Manager, my boss, asked me to find out what weight carton you were using to ship those pamphlets, you told me your people had selected a No. 10 cardboard weighing three ounces. The Department Manager told me to tell you to drop that down to a No. 6 paperboard. No wonder we're running so high on our postage."

D. "Pete didn't seem to really understand how to boot the new computer we got. So I went ahead and made up this checklist that I think you'll find useful in training him and other new operators on that process."

E. "I see Tillie and Sam are at it again, bickering all the time. Switch Sam with Joan to get him away from Tillie."

Today, Otto has plenty of time to check out new operators as the computer is shut down because management hasn't arranged for the new program to be delivered yet. In addition, revision of plant- wide supply procedures has not yet been approved by management, and Otto can't get supplies because procurement won't honor the old charge numbers which expired at midnight last night!

Questions
(about XYZ Company Case):

1. In items "A" and "B", is the Section Manager:

   ___ managing?

   or

   ___ supervising?

What determined your answer? (Check all that apply)

   ___ He was worrying about mission work.

   ___ He was bypassing the Supervisor and giving workers orders directly.

   ___ He was concerned with specific methods and techniques by which mission work should be done.

   ___ His concern for mission work was not in terms of resources and long-range planning.

   Other _____

   _____.

2. In items "C", "D", and "E", although never violating the chain-of-command, what are both the Section Manager and the Superintendent doing:

___ managing?

or

___ supervising?

What determined your answer? (Check all that apply)

___ They were worrying about mission work.

___ They bypassed the Supervisor and gave direct orders to the workers.

___ They were concerned about specific methods and techniques by which mission work should be done.

___ Their concern for mission work was not in terms of resources and long-range planning.

(Other)_____

14   The Organizational Role of the Supervisor

Answers to Exercise One
1. In items "A" and "B", is the Section Manager:

   ___ managing?

   or

   _X_ supervising?

   What determined your answer? (Check all that apply)

   _X_ He was worrying about mission work.

   _X_ He was bypassing the Supervisor and giving workers orders directly.

   _X_ He was concerned with specific methods and techniques by which mission work should be done.

   _X_ His concern for mission work was not in terms of resources and long-range planning.

   (Other) *He was not performing his managerial job.*

2. In items "C", "D", and "E", although never violating the chain-of-command, what are both Section Manager and the Department Manager doing:

   ___ managing?

   or

   _X_ supervising?

   What determined your answer? (Check all that apply)

   _X_ They were worrying about mission work.

   _X_ They bypassed the Supervisor and gave direct orders to the workers.

   _X_ They were concerned about specific methods and techniques by which mission work should be done.

   _X_ Their concern for mission work was not in terms of resources and long-range planning.

   (Other) *They both failed to provide the needed resources for the job.*

Exercise Two

Donna's company has a supervisory training program which teaches that supervisors should "manage;" that is, not get involved in day-to-day operating details, but spend their time doing forward planning, setting overall goals for the workgroup, and reviewing progress at periodic intervals rather than as work is going on.

As a result, Donna finds out about mistakes, late deliveries, problems with other units, and off-target progress at periodic review meetings with her workers, or through complaints from other supervisors or her own workers. Occasionally she discovers something has gone wrong when her boss or her boss's boss calls to ask why. Usually she doesn't know, and has to do some detective work to find out.

Donna has great plans and goals agreed to by her workers, but they are beginning to feel Donna used these to get the workers to agree to work harder because she never seems to be there to provide help when needed. Therefore, workers butt their heads against the wall trying to work with inadequate supplies or lack of cooperation from other groups, and Donna doesn't get around to doing anything about it until things have gone on like that for a while. In addition, Donna's boss sometimes finds that workers are puzzled about what to do when faced with certain problems, or are not sure how to do their work when a procedure has been changed. The boss has stepped in several times to straighten out the workers. He is also increasingly disturbed that Donna doesn't have answers on the tip of her tongue when he wants to find out something about a particular piece of work going through her unit.

Donna's response is "I'm paid to manage, not get wrapped up in details. My job is to set goals with my people, then leave them free to meet those goals unless they run into problems. I know when my help is needed by the production reports that come out weekly, or by complaints from other departments. If my workers need my help, they have only to come tell me...my door is always open. I should be involved with budgets, manpower planning, and looking ahead to next year, not worrying about today's work."

Questions
(about Donna's Company):

1. What is wrong with Donna "managing by exception" (that is, stepping in to find out what's going on only when a problem occurs)?

2. What are the effects of Donna using periodic meetings, weekly production reports, complaints from other units, and her "open door" to find out when things aren't going as they should?

3. What effect did Donna's lack of attention to details have on her boss doing his/her own job?

Answers to Exercise Two

1. What is wrong with Donna "managing by exception" (that is, stepping in to find out what's going on only when a problem occurs)?

   Problems are discovered after the fact

2. What are the effects of Donna using periodic meetings, weekly production reports, complaints from other units, and her "open door" to find out when things aren't going as they should?

   Mission workers find her approach as a means to get more work out without any help. She lacks credibility in the eyes of her mission workers.

3. What effect did Donna's lack of attention to details have on her boss doing his/her own job?

   Her boss felt the need to "straighten out" the mission workers. She lacked credibility in the eyes of her boss.

Exercise Three
The County Hospital Case

Supervisors in the two technical labs have been having troubles with the computer department. It seems the computer was set up originally to serve the accounting and business office, so accounting and business has first priority. As a result, computer analyses of lab reports are slow in coming back, and lab people often stand around because they can't go ahead with some of their work until the analyses arrive. In addition, the computer schedulers always seem to be in meetings whenever the lab supervisors want to get something through on a "rush" priority.

Each of the lab supervisors has chosen a different approach to the problem, as described below:

1. Chase has decided he'll never get the computer schedulers to respond to his needs. So, Chase has set up a procedure for getting his reports into the computer right away. He hand carries the lab report to the computer department. If a scheduler is there, Chase gives him/her a real sales pitch to get the work marked "RUSH". If a scheduler is not there, Chase stamps it "RUSH" himself, then he hand-carries the report to the programmers and stands there until he is sure they started work on it.

Chase has delegated one of his workers to pick up the program when it is finished, carry it to computer operations, and then go pick up the finished data runs when they come off the computer. This avoids the analyses sitting in a corner until someone from computers or mail service gets around to delivering them.

Chase gets the job done. His group never waits for information or reports from other departments, because he goes and gets them. They never lack for materials, because Chase "RUSHES" everything through procurement, or goes and "appropriates" it from another department.

18 The Organizational Role of the Supervisor

2. Layton has also decided he'll never be able to count on the computer schedulers. He has thrown up his hands and said, "The hospital can't hold me accountable for results if I don't have control over the people who are supposed to serve me. If they'd just give me my own computer, or at least my own scheduler, then maybe I could get something done."

As a result, Layton's lab is always late. The workers often do not have enough equipment. Layton says, "When you have to rely on people who serve other priorities, there's not much you can do about it.", because Layton's purchase orders follow the normal routine and often get set aside when something "RUSH" comes in.

Layton's solution is to just let the problem happen. If things get bad enough, perhaps management will get the message and give him the control he wants.

Questions
(about County Hospital Case):

1. Whose solution seems the better to you? Why?

2. If the hospital were to remove Layton, what reasons might they give?

3. If the hospital were to remove Chase, what reasons might they give?

4. What is the Supervisor's real responsibility; to get the job done, or to get the job done through the organization provided? Why?

Answers to Exercise Three

1. Whose solution seems the better to you? Why?

   Neither one

2. If the hospital were to remove Layton, what reasons might they give?

   Not getting the work out on time

3. If the hospital were to remove Chase, what reasons might they give?

   Not using the proper methods to receive services from other units.

4. What is the Supervisor's real responsibility; to get the job done, or to get the job done through the organization provided? Why?

   To get the job done through the organization provided, because:
   1) The organization must operate properly, not just one unit.
   2) There should be no duplicate efforts.
   3) Meeting one unit's objective should not create problems for another unit.

Exercise Four -- What Supervision is....
Who? And Why?

The Supervisor's Position on the Management Team
(Circle T for True or F for False Statement.)

In order to play the rightful role in a distinct position on the management team, the Supervisor must:

T F 1. Recognize that the whole management structure, including managers and supervisors, should focus its time and attention on the same goal: Seeing that the work gets out.

T F 2. Be involved with technical details such as: How the work should be done; how it is being done; how the equipment is designed to function; what the equipment is capable of; and whether a given piece of work will meet quality standards and schedules when it is finished.

T F 3. Accept that both managers and supervisors should deal directly with workers on such crucial issues as: Assuring safe work habits; meeting quality and schedule requirements on key work assignments; and policing worker adherence to rules, policies, and procedures.

T F 4. Realize that on critical issues like safety, money or labor relations, staff offices (like safety, personnel, or the controller) are more responsible than the supervisor for what workers do.

T F 5. Realize that while supervising is different from the work workers do, it is basically the same kind of work managers do.

T F 6. Be just as knowledgeable about how workers should do their work as the manager is.

T F 7. Develop just as much understanding about how worker errors or accidents occur as managers have.

T F 8. Have complete authority over his/her workers, and over the allocation of services and resources they call on to get their work done.

T F 9. Expect the managers to play their rightful role, that of day-to-day coordination of other units with the supervisor's unit.

T F 10. Get the job done, even if it means repeatedly handling an activity personally, which a service group has been derelict in providing, or delegating one of his/her workers to carry out that service.

Answers to Exercise Four --
What Supervision is....Who? And why?

The Supervisor's Position on the Management Team

In order to play the rightful role in a distinct position on the management team, the supervisor must:

T/F 1. Recognize that the whole management structure, including managers and supervisors, should focus its time and attention on the same goal: Seeing that the work gets out. [T]

T/F 2. Be involved with technical details such as: How the work should be done; how it is being done; how the equipment is designed to function; what the equipment is capable of; and whether a given piece of work will meet quality standards and schedules when it is finished. [F]

T/F 3. Accept that both managers and supervisors should deal directly with workers on such crucial issues as: Assuring safe work habits; meeting quality and schedule requirements on key work assignments; and policing worker adherence to rules, policies, and procedures. [T]

T/F 4. Realize that on critical issues like safety, money or labor relations, staff offices (like safety, personnel, or the controller) are more responsible than the supervisor for what workers do. [F]

T/F 5. Realize that while supervising is different from the work workers do, it is basically the same kind of work managers do. [T]

T/F 6. Be just as knowledgeable about how workers should do their work as the manager is. [T]

T/F 7. Develop just as much understanding about how worker errors or accidents occur as managers have. [T]

T/F 8. Have complete authority over his/her workers, and over the allocation of services and resources they call on to get their work done.

T/F 9. Expect the managers to play their rightful role, that of day-to-day coordination of other units with the supervisor's unit.

T/F 10. Get the job done, even if it means repeatedly handling an activity personally, which a service group has been derelict in providing, or delegating one of his/her workers to carry out that service.

CHAPTER 2

The Supervisor as Head-of-Workgroup

In the previous chapter, we indicated that a supervisor exists to see that the work does get out. The functions include responsibilities in the following broad areas of responsibility:

1. Quantity of work put out (concern for schedules, volume of work or service)

2. Quality of group's work (concern for end product, employee performance, service to others, accuracy, etc.)

3. Cost control (helping to set, and/or operate within budgets)

4. Cost improvement (concern for finding easier, faster, less expensive ways of doing work, or providing more service per dollar)

5. Safety (concern for accident prevention, even in sedentary, low risk operations)

Managers exist to see the work can get out. This difference is significant for effective operation of any organization.

The supervisor is that member of the management team paid to be concerned about the performance, behavior, and interactions of mission workers. This requirement adds three additional functions to the list of supervisory responsibilities as follows:

6. Lateral coordination (integrating your group's efforts with other workgroups)

7. Rules, policies, and procedures (concern for updating, developing, and enforcing)

8. Personnel matters

    A. Selecting and hiring

    B. Orientation and training

    C. Performance counselling

    D. Discipline

    E. Termination and layoffs

These eight areas are common to all supervisors regardless of the kind of business. Some have additional responsibilities based on their areas of specialty such as customer relations, public relations, security, etc. These broad areas of responsibility are shared by both supervisors and managers. Therefore, these broad areas do not designate the work of the supervisor. This can only be done by looking within each broad area at specific duties which should be unique to supervisors. For example: The supervisor should inform workers what the quality standards are, whereas the manager must negotiate with clients and other departments to establish overall quality standards. (For a complete list of supervisory tasks, refer to "*Duties of First-Line Supervisors,*"

PMI, Box 8789, Calabasas, CA 91302-8789. This booklet identifies supervisory duties in detail.)

Some sample duties are:

1. Quantity
   A. Inform employees of job requirements and schedules, and involve them in defining work methods.

   B. Have alternative courses of action for likely emergencies.

   C. Get an early lead on critical items.

2. Quality
   A. Keep quality changes up-to-date.

   B. Train employees in importance of meeting quality standards.

   C. Spot-check work in progress and completed work for acceptability.

3. Cost Control
   A. Communicate approved budgets to employees and plan with them how to comply.

   B. Let workers know the unit costs of supplies and materials they use, as an aid in making them cost conscious.

   C. Recommend changes to make it less time consuming, more accurate, etc.

4. Cost Improvement
   A. Solicit suggestions from your employees for increased efficiency and cost improvement.

   B. Monitor improvements after installation and revise as needed to produce better results.

   C. Learn techniques of work analysis and work simplification.

5. Safety
   A. Identify the types of hazards common in the kind of work you supervise.

   B. Enforce safety rules.

   C. Occasionally practice emergency procedures with your workers.

6. Rules, policies, and procedures
   A. Know the rules, policies, and procedures, and keep informed of changes or interpretations.

   B. Inform employees of new rules, policies, procedure changes, and tell them the "whys."

   C. Set a good example in following rules, policies, and procedures yourself.

7. Personnel matters
A. Selecting and hiring
   1. Review work methods and workloads to determine if a vacancy really needs to be filled.

   2. Consider qualifications of your own people before asking for authority to hire.

B. Orientation and training
   1. Review with employees the orientation given to them by personnel.

   2. Review training plans with both trainer and trainee

C. Performance counselling
   1. Discuss formal evaluation with manager before counselling employee.

   2. Document actions taken to help poor employees come up to standard.

D. Discipline
   1. Inform manager if problem persists and of the action that you would recommend be taken.
   2. Be prepared for and take part in grievance hearings.

E. Termination
   1. Assure your position in accordance with policy or contract.
   2. Confer with management on proposed action.

There are multitudes of skills necessary to perform these vital supervisory duties. A supervisor must always target some self-improvement programs for sharpening his/her skills.

Summary
Chapter Two

There are three major functions an effective supervisor performs for the organization. The first is:

Head of Workgroup

A supervisor performs specific tasks in eight broad areas of responsibilities. These eight are common to all supervisors. However, there may be other responsibilities which are unique to the job. The eight common areas are as follows:

1. Quantity of work
2. Quality of work
3. Cost control
4. Cost improvement
5. Safety
6. Lateral coordination
7. Rules, policies, and procedures
8. Personnel matters
    A. Selection and hiring
    B. Orientation and training
    C. Performance counselling
    D. Discipline
    E. Termination and layoffs

Exercises

In the following exercises there are no right or wrong answers. Therefore, no "correct" answers are given. You should respond to these questions for clarification of ideas for your own self-improvement.

Exercise One
The Ideal Supervisor

Kenny Dewett has just been appointed to supervise a workgroup which has not had a good record:

- -- Costs are higher than those of any similar operation in the organization.
- -- Quality is at an all-time low because emphasis has been on volume of output rather than on accuracy of work.
- -- In spite of the emphasis on volume, work is frequently behind schedule, resulting in a lot of "panic" and constant scrambling to try to get three or four jobs done at once. New work either has to wait, or else is crammed in, thus disrupting work currently in progress.
- -- In this confusion, attention to safety procedures has become lax; several accidents have occurred, although, fortunately, not resulting in injuries to anyone.

Since Kenny is coming in fresh from another operation, he wants to set things straight as soon as possible, and make up for the shortcomings the previous supervisor had allowed.

Questions
(about The Ideal Supervisor):

1. Of all the supervisor duties you have looked at on the previous pages, pick what you consider to be the two most important for Kenny to institute right away for each of the following goals: (Indicate duties by letter and numbers such as *5-A, 7-C-2*. See page 27.)

A. To get the group cost-conscious: (2 duties) _____ and _____.

B. To set a new tone for quality: (2 duties) _____ and _____.

C. To get schedules and output under control: (2 duties) _____ and _____.

D. To generate more attention to safety: (2 duties) _____ and _____.

2. What do you consider the most important duties for Kenny to perform in order to maintain good results in the following areas.

A. Quality: _____.
B. Quantity: _____.
C. Cost (control and improvement): _____.
D. Safety: _____.

3. Of the duties you listed in questions No. 1 and No. 2 above, which ones do you, personally, need to emphasize more than you have in the past?

Exercise Two
The Realities of Life

May Aswell is a conscientious supervisor. She has gone through the lists of supervisory duties, and she has, under each major area of responsibility, listed more duties.

Her list is quite large. May realized that she had previously been performing only about 60 percent of them, but when she reviewed the lists she had to admit that most of the duties were things she should be doing.

In several instances, May found that her boss was performing those duties which May now feels should be part of her job instead. For example, May felt she should be:

-- More involved in the hiring of new people for her own workgroup, therefore she checked "interview prospective candidates and recommend choices to manager" as part of her job.

-- The one to initiate and administer disciplinary actions.

-- Involved in helping the manager arrive at new policies, rules, or procedures. Therefore, she checked "recommend changes in policies as needed", and she added "be consulted by manager while new rules, policies, or procedures are still in the formative stages."

Surprisingly, her manager agreed with everything May had checked. So far, so good, everyone in agreement on what May should be doing.

However, 3 months later, nothing has changed!

May is still performing only about 60 percent of the duties she had checked. There have been no new hires and no disciplinary actions have come up, so we don't know if her manager will let her do what they agreed she should. She has yet to be consulted by her boss on new rules, policies, or procedures, and there have been three of those sent down in the last six weeks.

Questions
(about The Realities of Life):

1. We don't have information on what has caused May's inability to perform up to the ideal she and her boss had agreed upon, but if this had taken place in your own organization, which of the following causes do you feel would have been most likely:

(Check all that apply)

___ A. Too much "mission" work for supervisor to handle personally, leaving little time left for supervising.

___ B. Manager's discussions with supervisor focus mainly on work and output problems, with little or no time given to how the supervisor is doing on supervision.

___ C. Manager unwilling to let go, resulting in lack of confidence in supervisor.

___ D. Too much pressure on getting the work out, thus emphasizing only the most cruicial duties, leaving no time for others.

___ E. Certain areas of responsibility are "idealistic," and get no attention from managers or supervisors unless something bad happens.

___ F. Manager keeps calling meetings, which disrupt supervisor's ability to plan ahead.

___ G. Manager agrees to full range of duties for the supervisor, but only emphasizes a few crucial ones with the supervisor.

___ H. Manager sees supervisor as the "technical expert," so most discussions center around the work technology rather than supervision.

___ I. The manager is the real head-of-workgroup, tending to do many of the duties the supervisor should be doing.

___ J. Supervisor lacks skill or training at doing many of the duties, so emphasizes those with which he or she is comfortable.

___ K. Other

_____
_____.

2. In view of the items you checked above as being characteristic in your own organization, what action would you recommend to May that might enable her to do more of what she considers her supervisory job to be:

(Check all that apply)

___ A. Forget it. Things will always be as they have been. Just keep doing what you have been doing and don't worry about those other duties you think you should perform. You will never get to them anyway.

___ B. Resolve to get better organized so you can do more in the future.

___ C. Talk to your manager to see what the manager suggests.

___ D. Talk to your manager, identify the duties you just can't seem to get around to. Identify the reasons why and suggest solutions.

___ E. Set a target for adding just one of the new duties at a time, rather than trying to be perfect all at once.

___ F. Get some training in the duties in which you are not skilled.

___ G. Other

_____
_____
_____

CHAPTER 3

Coordinator with Other Supervisors

It is a supervisor's job to coordinate the policy interpretations of that supervisor's own unit with other supervisors. Policy interpretation of one supervisor may be different from the policy interpretation of another supervisor. Not resolving these differences between two supervisors could have negative impact on mission workers of both units.

The next issue in lateral coordination is to integrate the work of your workgroup with the work of other groups. Any slow-down or speed-up in your workgroup will have impact on other service units or units that depend on your workgroup's output. Adjustments in work output should be integrated with other unit supervisors.

Final requirements for an effective lateral coordination requires you to utilize the organization as designed. It is not acceptable to get together with two or three other supervisors and devise a system to bypass another unit just because that unit does not provide services on time. If you are not getting the right service, you should attempt to get the services on time.

The following is a description of different kinds of supervisors you may have interaction with in your organization.

Your Fellow Supervisors

"Operating" Supervisors

A. Supervisors who, along with you, report to the same boss.

B. Supervisors who report directly to a different boss, but whose workgroups do the same work as yours, except on a different shift or in a different area of the facility.

C. Supervisors who report directly to a different boss, but whose workgroups are next-in-line after your group in the sequential flow of your mission work. (i.e., Their groups receive materials, hardware, information, documents, etc. from your group on which your group has already completed its part of the work. These groups cannot continue the work properly unless your group has done its part correctly.)

D. Supervisors who report directly to a different boss, but whose workgroups immediately precede yours in the flow of your mission work. (i.e., Your group receives materials, hardware, information, documents, etc. from these groups on which these groups have already completed their part of the work. Your group cannot continue the work properly unless these groups have done their part correctly.)

"Service" Supervisors

E. Supervisors whose workgroups exist to provide support services to other groups. These groups do not perform work that is part of your mission work, but they do things for you that, if your group were to do them for themselves, would divert time and attention away from your mission work. (i.e., These groups provide supplies, plans, programs, procedures, or services so that your group can concentrate primarily on its mission work.)

"Staff" Supervisors

F. Supervisors of staff groups who provide advice or policy guidance to you on the running of your workgroup, or who monitor and report on your group's performance.

Improved coordination will prevent future problems and will eliminate your boss's need to do a supervisory task of coordination. However, there are times when your manager should get involved. These occassions are characterized by the following:

1. When you and another supervisor cannot agree.

2. When you and another supervisor agree on a solution which goes beyond your authority.

3. When the decision you and another supervisor reach can leave your boss left out of the informational chain and/or catch your manager unaware of your decision when higher management asks your manager a question.

Keys to Lateral Coordination Among "Operating" Supervisors

1. *Understanding each others' functions and problems.* Each supervisor is required to understand other groups functions and problems. This understanding can come because you have worked in other units or you have had a personal working knowledge of other units. However, there may be several other groups where you don't understand their functions and problems. You can visit their operations and have that unit's supervisor show you around, ask to sit in their staff meetings, read their job descriptions, have coffee or lunch with the unit supervisor and ask the supervisor to describe some of their functions. You should also

get your workgroup informed of other group's functions and problems.

2. *Building bridges to cooperation*. The best time to show cooperation with other units is when there is no conflict, no problem, no need. When you need cooperation, there is no time to build cooperation. Cooperation can be achieved much more easily when:

* You have given the other supervisor advance notice.
* You have cooperated with the other supervisor sometime in the past.
* You are always honest about the urgency of your problem.
* You have recognized "bridges to cooperation" are built during informal, non-crisis contacts.
* You anticipate problems which might affect other groups.
* You share information on what is going on in your group with other supervisors.

In order for you to consciously plan contact with other supervisors, we have provided a tool we call "conscious-contact planner." Use this form to record who you have contacted in the previous eight weeks and who you want to contact in the next eight weeks. After you have identified the individuals and the times, plan a specific approach from our suggestions under "Building Bridges to Cooperation." Then, when you meet with that individual, use the approch best suited to you and to the occasion.

Coordinating with "Service" Supervisors

Typically, "service" groups are those that exist to do something for other units, enabling other units to focus more of their time and attention on doing the work they exist to perform.
Obvious examples:

CONSCIOUS-CONTACT PLANNER

NAMES | **WEEKS** →

| | 8 | 7 | 6 | 5 | 4 | 3 | 2 | 1 | 1 | 2 | 3 | 4 | 5 | 6 | 7 | 8 |

Today

Accounting

Maintenance

Personnel

Purchasing

Supply

These units are not:

* "Line" units, which perform the "mission" of the overall organization.
* "Staff" units, which provide advice or consultation.
* "Control" units, which exist to tell other units what to do, rather than provide a service for them.

You can develop a list of "service" groups in your organization. Then, classify them under four catagories according to the quality and timeliness of service that you receive:

1) Always: _____(no need for improvement)

2) Usually:_____

3) Rarely:_____

4) Almost never:_____

How to get "Service" and Strengthen the Organization

If you find you frequently do not get the quality or timeliness of service you feel you should get, there are various alternatives open to you:

1. See if you can determine the causes and try to work out a solution with the service supervisor, or with other supervisors who also use that service, such as:

   A. Suggest ways the service supervisor might improve operation of the service group.

   B. Ask if there are ways you can operate in your own group which will ease the service supervisor's difficulties and get you better service.

   C. Offer to lend the service supervisor people or resources to help them with better service.

   D. See if you can coordinate your demands on the service group with other supervisors who also use that service.

2. Recommend to your boss any changes in organization or procedures which you and the service supervisor agree are needed to improve service.

3. Go to bat, for the service supervisor, with the service supervisor's boss to request more resources for the service group, if that will ease the problem.

One method of determining the difficulties a service group faces in giving you the kind of service you want, when you want it, is called role reversal. That is when you mentally put yourself in the service supervisor's place and force yourself to answer:

A. As the Service Supervisor:

1. What is the group's real mission and just what are we trying to accomplish?

2. From what do we get our satisfaction as "professionals?"

3. What restrictions, constraints, or conflicting goals has upper management imposed on us?

4. On what is my boss judging me? (How well we serve other groups, or how efficiently we operate internally?)

5. What do the supervisors or workgroups who use our service characteristically do that makes it tough for us to do a good job?

B. As yourself:

6. What might I do to improve the situation? For example:

   a. Make sure the service supervisor knows the real urgency, priority, or seriousness of my problem each time I request service.

   b. If my own group is guilty of any of the answers to Question 5, modify the way we operate if possible.

7. If the problem is limited resources in the service group, how can I help convince the service supervisor's boss to give the service group what they need?

8. Can I get together with other supervisors who use the service to coordinate the demands and priorities among us, so the service group doesn't have to make the decision as to whose work is the most important?

C. Discuss your answers with the service supervisor.

If you are a "Service" Supervisor

1. "Market" your group's services.

2. Keep in touch with reality. (Get out where the action is).

3. Go to bat to win system changes that ease pressures and conflicts faced by "user" supervisors.

4. When requests for your services are in priority conflict, get the mutual boss of the supervisors in conflict to resolve the priority. (This is not a contradiction to what we have said so far. When the problem is a priority conflict it should be resolved by the common boss.)

Your role as a supervisor is to get the service you require, and at the same time, strengthen the organization.

Suppose: The supervisor from whom you are trying to get cooperation or service remains uncooperative, or proves to be incompetent.

What should you do now?

___ A. Give up and proceed without help, or "bootleg" in some other way.

___ B. "Blow the whistle" to his/her boss.

___ C. Go to your boss, and recommend what you think should be done at a higher level to get the other supervisor's boss to do something about the problem.

___ D. Get all the other supervisors together who are also having trouble with that person, and try to come up with a group recommendation.

Of course, as you will realize, options A and B are not appropriate. Therefore, you may want to take either C or D, or both options, depending on your preference.

Exercises

The Service Supervisor's Role

The Work Improvement Group is a three-person unit supervised by Wright. The group exists to help supervisors throughout the organization make improvements in their workgroup's procedures, workplace layout, work methods, and so forth. This is not an industrial engineering group which designs major process changes, but is concerned with day-to-day improvements in efficiency of the kind a supervisor could make on his/her own authority.

The group was established to help supervisors, but when Wright took over, this is what he inherited:

1. The group usually found out about a supervisor considering a change after the change had already been made. In almost every case, the group found that if they had just been called in at the beginning, they could have helped save a great deal more. But they found the supervisor defensively hostile to any further improvements they might suggest.

2. At the end of each month, the group has to report to headquarters all simplifications installed by supervisors, and the savings accrued. However, with limited staff, the group could not go out and collect the data themselves, so Wright's predecessor had gotten higher management to order supervisors to report installed new methods to the group at the end of each month.

Because month-end is a supervisor's busiest time, the directive from management did not solve the problem. Very few supervisors submitted the reports on time. So Wright`s predecessor usually spent the last week of each month out in the operation, badgering supervisors or asking their managers to tell supervisors to get the reports in.

3. Each quarter, the roles were reversed. Supervisors have cost and efficiency objectives they must meet each quarter. So, the last two weeks of every third month, the group was always hit with a flood of requests to come down and help find improvements.

It was impossible to handle the load, so the group served supervisors on a "first-come, first-served" basis. This resulted in many not getting help in time to meet their quarterly goals, and others complaining that their high-priority operations lost out to less-important departments who got their requests in earlier.

To make sure they got help when wanted, accounting set up their own part-time improvement group and never called on the official one.

However, Wright has straightened this all out. Now lots of requests for help are coming in well ahead of the time they'll be needed, and the group is being called in at the beginning of improvements. The monthly reports are being submitted by supervisors regularly. Supervisors are acting on methods improvements during each quarter, instead of just at the end. Priority conflicts for the group's services are being resolved with no hard-feelings, and without supervisors suffering for not meeting their bosses' demands, and Wright has added no people! Neither have any of the supervisors! It has all been done through better coordination.

Questions
(about The Work Simplification Group):

1. What do you suppose Wright did to "market" the group's services, so supervisors would want to call him in early instead of going ahead without him?

(Check all that apply)

____ A. He got top management to order supervisors to call the group whenever considering making an improvement.

____ B. He publicized to all supervisors the successes of the few who did call him in early.

____ C. When successes were publicized or reported, he made sure the Supervisor (not the group) got the credit.

____ D. He and his people got out into the operations and made frequent contact with supervisors who should have been using the group's services.

____ E. Other

_____
_____.

2. Initially, the monthly report from supervisors met resistance because it came at the supervisors' busiest time. How do you suppose Wright overcame this resistance.?

(Check all that apply)

____ A. He got top management to threaten penalties for any supervisor who failed to submit the report on time.

___ B. He got top management to change due dates to the early part of each month, when supervisors' other workloads were the lightest.

___ C. He convinced supervisors that, if they called the group in early on potential improvements, the group would thus have been involved in what the report covers, and could do a lot of the report themselves.

___ D. By getting the due date changed, and by showing supervisors the group could help with the report, he got supervisors to see the group as a helpful resource rather than an imposed interference.

___ E. Other

_____

_____.

3. At the end of each quarter, a flood of requests for the group's service comes from supervisors. Since there is limited time to process these requests, they have to be put in some sort of priority. It turned out that "first-come, first-served" was not a good way, as very-important units sometimes didn't get served because their requests came in later than requests from less-important units, and high-urgency projects often had to wait behind low-urgency projects.

Who should set the priority?

(Check all that apply)

___ A. Wright and/or his boss.

___ B. Each supervisor by himself/herself or with his/her own boss.

___ C. The higher level boss to whom the supervisors in conflict ultimately report.

___ D. The supervisors in conflict, themselves.

___ E. Other

_____

_____.

4. Although, ideally, supervisors in conflict should resolve the priorities among themselves. Wright found this often didn't work because supervisors were under pressure from their immediate bosses, each of whom had his/her own priorities. Supervisors shouldn't change priorities without the boss' approval, and immediate bosses weren't likely to give in. So, instead of sending supervisors back to resolve conflicts themselves, Wright began "fronting for them" with the higher-level manager to determine which should be serviced first, and to adjust the demands on supervisors accordingly.

What reaction do you suppose this caused among supervisors?

(Check all that apply)

___A. They felt Wright was sticking his nose in where it was none of his business.

___B. They felt Wright was on their side, trying to get the pressures on them reduced if he couldn't serve them right away.

___C. They found they didn't have to lie about the urgency of their work to get service, and that their bosses were more tolerant if a project got delayed for a while in deference to higher-priority work.

___D. They and their bosses could unite to convince higher management to give Wright more resources if priority conflicts could not be resolved by the manager to whom they ultimately report.

___ E. Other

_____

_____.

Answers
(about The Work Improvement Group)

1. What do you suppose Wright did to "market" the group's services, so supervisors would want to call him in early instead of going ahead without him?

(Check all that apply)

___A. He got top management to order supervisors to call the group whenever considering making an improvement.

_X_ B. He publicized to all supervisors the successes of the few who did call him in early.

_X_ C. When successes were publicized or reported, he made sure the supervisor (not the group) got the credit.

_X_ D. He and his people got out into the operations and made frequent contact with supervisors who should have been using the group's services.

___ E. Other

_____

_____.

2. Initially, the monthly report from supervisors met resistance because it came at a supervisor's busiest time. How do you suppose Wright overcame this resistance.

(Check all that apply)

___ A. He got top management to threaten penalties for any supervisor who failed to submit the report on time.

_X_ B. He got top management to change due dates to the early part of each month when supervisors' other workloads were the lightest.

_X_ C. He convinced supervisors that, if they called the group in early on potential improvements, the group would thus have been involved in what the report covers and could do a lot of the report themselves.

_X_ D. By getting the due date changed and by showing supervisors the group could help with the report, he got supervisors to see the group as a helpful resource rather than an imposed interference.

___ E. Other

_____

_____.

3. At the end of each quarter, a flood of requests for the group's service comes from supervisors. Since there is limited time to process these requests, they have to be put in some sort of priority. It turned out that "first-come, first-served" was not a good way, as very-important units sometimes didn't get served because their requests came in later than requests from less-important units; and high-urgency projects often had to wait behind low-urgency projects.

Who should set the priority?

(Check all that apply)

___ A. Wright and/or his boss.

___ B. Each supervisor by himself or with his/her own boss.

_X_ C. The higher level boss to whom the supervisors in conflict ultimately all report.

_X_ D. The supervisors in conflict, themselves. (Ideal)

___ E. Other

_____

_____.

4. Although, ideally, supervisors in conflict should resolve the priorities among themselves. Wright found this often didn't work because supervisors were under pressure from their immediate bosses, each of whom had his/her own priorities. Supervisors shouldn't change priorities without the boss' approval, and immediate bosses weren't likely to give it. So, instead of sending supervisors back to resolve conflicts themselves, Wright began "fronting for them" with the higher-level manager to determine which should be serviced first, and to adjust the demands on supervisors accordingly.

What reaction do you suppose this caused among supervisors?

(Check all that apply)

___ A. They felt Wright was sticking his nose in where it was none of his business.

_X_ B. They felt Wright was on their side, trying to get the pressures on them reduced if he couldn't serve them right away.

_X_ C. They found they didn't have to lie about urgency of their work to get service and that their bosses were more tolerant if a project got delayed for a while in deference to higher-priority work.

58 The Organizational Role of the Supervisor

    _X_ D. They and their bosses could unite to convince higher management to give Wright more resources if priority conflicts could not be resolved by the manager to whom they ultimately report.

    ___ E. Other

_____

_____.

CHAPTER 4

Supervisor as a Member-of-Management

Supervisors must be considered as participating members-of-management. That means that a supervisor is not just a person who receives signals from management, but rather someone who participates in the decisions involved in giving the signal. Often this function is misunderstood. Possibly this is the most difficult function of a supervisor in an organization. In some organizations, the supervisor is utilized as a "buffer" between managers and mission workers, protecting the manager from the demands of mission workers. In other organizations, the supervisor is looked upon as a "shock absorber," cushioning the harshness of management decisions for the mission workers, or, the supervisor is used as the "filling in a sandwich" chewed on by both managers and mission workers! But, rightfully, a supervisor must be someone who represents management to workers. That means, when the workers hear from supervisors, they know that they are hearing from management.

Also, a supervisor must represent workers to management. Management must be assured that when the supervisor talks about mission workers, the supervisor represents mission workers fairly.

Research shows that in every unit of work, productivity is high when workers see the supervisor as an image of influence. Influence with management.

Conversely, output is low when workers see their supervisor as a "flunky", someone who has no say-so with management. A supervisor can be robbed of this image of influence by three means:

1. Supervisor doing it to himself/herself. Demonstrating that the Supervisor has no say-so.

2. Supervisors allowing other units to dictate to their workers.

3. Managers bypassing the chain-of-communication.

A supervisor is paid to be a member-of-management. This function requires that you avoid being looked upon by your workgroup as a "flunky."

I. How to Keep from Becoming a "Flunky" by Your Own Actions

The effect of a supervisor who obviously has no "clout" upstairs is that the workers will start worrying about who can look out for their interests. Therefore, you must avoid fighting too many losing battles. You should make the decision yourself if you already know what the answer will be. Also, to demonstrate to workers that you have "clout" upstairs, you should recommend a decision to management, only on those issues where you feel strongly that the recommendation is in management's best interests.

When an employee asks for special exceptions, or changes in rules or procedures, you can show that you are part of the "management team" by:

A. Making the decision yourself when you already know what policy is.

B. Taking the request to higher management when you feel it has merit.

C. Telling the employee, after getting a ruling from higher management, that "we" decided "yes" or "no."

When you disagree with a policy or procedure higher management is passing down, you should voice that disagreement to your boss before announcing the policy. If your boss does not agree with your point of view, tell employees "We decided...."

II. How to Keep Other Units From Making You A "Flunky".

When changes are made with your workgroup as a result of work orders or changes given directly to your mission workers, you should resist "staff" direction. Make your own decisions. Consider their input as advice rather than direction. You should also insist that "staff" groups resolve any conflicts in priorities or procedures at their own level, or with your boss. You could allow "staff" contact with your employees only for specific activities you have previously approved, but not for:

--Changes in policies or procedures.

--Introducing new programs.

--Direction on work methods.

III. Your Manager Can Make You Look Like A "Flunky" When:

--Your manager bypasses you and gives orders directly to your workers.

--Your manager tells workers to follow instructions different from those previously given by you.

--Your manager allows employees to come directly to him/her without your knowledge.

--Your manager reverses decisions already announced by you.

--Your manager does not include you in planning sessions affecting your workgroup.

--Your manager does not seek your ideas on new procedures or policies.

--Your manager doesn't credit you with first-hand knowledge of work situation and considers his/her own knowledge superior and doesn't listen to you.

A major complaint of supervisors is that they do not feel management (their boss in combination with their boss' bosses) will back them up.

If you make a decision, your management should back you up when:

1. You are right and everyone agrees.

2. You are right, but top management disagrees (management must give you a full explanation for their disagreement).

3. You are right, but a customer disagrees (an explanation should be given for keeping the customer happy).

4. You are right but the union (or some other powerful interest group) disagrees (again, with an explanation to you).

5. You are wrong, but your decision was made with the organization's best interests in mind, and you erred only in judgement (a clarification should be made so that you won't repeat that error in judgement).

6. There is no right or wrong, but your decision and judgement are questioned by powerful others. (The rationale must be given to you.)

   A. Your decision is a clear violation of rules, but was made because you felt that it was the lesser of two evils. (You must correct the decision and inform your workers of the change.)

   B. Your decision violates the law, exceeds your authority, or represents a total disregard for instructions from a higher authority.

If higher management reverses you on an appeal or grievance which has gone up through channels, they have failed to back you up if they tell you nothing but the decision. However, if they cue you in on their reasoning, and give you a chance to present your side of the issue personally, they have done the job correctly. But when higher management reverses one of your decisions, *you* should institute the change and announce it to your employees.

Organizations should operate without much distinction between the "management team" and the "worker team." We all belong to the same team, we just perform different tasks. Therefore, in order to strengthen the unity of this teamwork, you, the supervisor, should perform the same way with your mission workers as you would expect your boss to perform with you. That is, back your employees not just when they are right, but even when they are wrong, if their decision or action was made in good conscience with good intent for the best interest of the organization. When honest (not willful or negligent) mistakes are made, some of the responsibility is yours. Take the blame yourself.

Summary

Chapter Four

Representing Management to Workers

Serve as the primary link in the channel-of-communication, both downward and upward.

Identify and define for yourself management's viewpoint on policies.

Transmit management policies to workers, and reflect management's viewpoint. (Don't pass the buck.)

Follow up on application of policies transmitted.

Relay pertinent information on company progress, product plans, departmental plans, etc. to the group.

Identify what authority you can exercise without prior approval from above, and use that authority wherever possible to make decisions on employee requests without referring them to higher management.

Encourage your boss to follow the chain-of-command.

Stay alert to employee reactions in order to note where management policies may need modifications.

Participate with manager in defining procedures for your group, and make recommendations before the manager renders decisions which will affect your group.

Inform the boss of significant and potential problems, and offer proposed solutions.

Stand behind your manager's policies in your contacts outside your department.

Representing Workers to Management

As workers look upward into the organization, the first person they should see as a member of the management team is the supervisor.

As managers look downward, the first person they should see as part of the worker team is a mission worker, not the supervisor.

Although we refer to the management team and the worker team, we are not talking about two opposing teams. They are both only sub-units of the same team.

Supervisor as a Member-of-Management

Why Managers Sometimes do not Include Supervisors as "Members- of-Management"

A. They are not sure with whom the supervisor identifies. (Supervisors don't grasp management's objectives.)

B. Supervisors have "tunnel vision." (Supervisors don't have a management perspective.)

C. They are not sure about supervisors' judgement or knowledge.

D. Supervisors are repeatedly caught "wpd" (Apparently, supervisors don't know what's going on or they don't look ahead.)

E. Too many cries of "help" from supervisors. (They seem to want managers to do their job for them.) Managers need to see supervisors as being "on the management team," not on the workers team.

The supervisor should be that member of management who is paid to be knowledgeable of, and up-to-date on, a day-to-day basis on the specific methods and techniques by which mission workers:
* Do their work.
* Relate to each other and to other groups.
* Relate to rules, policies, and procedures.
* Express their ideas, feelings, and problems.
* Receive information from higher authority.

This is not the job of managers. Managers exist to manage the provision of resources and to plan for the future.

You will successfully represent your workgroup only when your manager sees no need to remain first-hand familiar with the details of your operation, and no need to do your work for you.

How to Gain (or maintain) Managers' Confidence in You as a Participating "Member-of-Management"

1. Provide information from your workgroup to help managers do their job. You should:

   A. Estimate on resources needed for upcoming workload or time period.

   B. Estimate on time needed (schedules) for upcoming work.

   C. Predict the future needs. (Estimates on resources, procedural changes, repairs, training, etc. that will be needed to avoid emergency problems downstream.)

D. Comment on how new policies, procedures, or organizational changes under consideration would affect your workgroup.

E. Recommend improvements in work methods.

F. Inform the manager on day-to-day progress, what's going on, likely problems, etc., anything the boss may need to plan ahead or coordinate at his/her own level.

2. Make sure that requested information and recommendations are process supported. For example, you should be able to make the following types of statements to qualify for process supported recommendations.

A. "Boss, here are the estimates. I've checked with Ms. X, Mr. Y, and Mrs. Z, and they all concur that the costs I've assigned to each item are accurate. In addition, I've checked the total by computer, and it adds up o.k."

B. "Boss, here are the estimates. To get them, I ran a little test with some new work methods in my workgroup. That test (which I've documented for you) showed we can get by with only a 9-1/2 percent increase over last year."

3. Make sure that volunteered information, recommendations, or requests are sensitive to managerial concerns.

A. Show with which team you identify.

B. Consider the organization's big picture from the manager's viewpoint.

C. Be sure to consider issues that your management is concerned about.

D. Make your prime objective in harmony with your manager's prime concern.

E. Whenever possible, make your own decision, and take care of your own coordination. Remember, a little publicity will never do you any harm. Let your manager know some of the actions you have taken.

F. Provide visibility to outstanding performance and talent within your group.

If a supervisor is not recognized as a part of the management team, both management and worker teams suffer.

This book is focused on the organizational role of a supervisor because that position is crucial to organizational effectiveness.

> No doubt there are a myriad of skills in human relations, communication, etc. needed to perform this job successfully. However, without knowing the role of a supervisor, the skills used may not produce the desired results.

Are you really a supervisor?
(A check list)

(Check only those to which you can answer "yes")

___ 1. Do your employees almost always come to you as their primary source of information about what's going on with upper management and about how rules, policies, procedures or benefits apply to them?

___ 2. Do upper management and staff departments use you almost always as the primary channel for communicating their messages to employees?

___ 3. Do you find the vast majority of questions, requests, suggestions, and complaints from employees can be handled by you without referring to higher management or a staff department for an answer or decision?

___ 4. Does your boss include you in planning discussions which affect the overall operations, not just your own unit?

___ 5. Does your boss consult you before finalizing plans, policies, or procedures which will affect your unit?

___ 6. Are your inputs sought and given weight when upper-management is considering raises, transfers, promotions, layoffs, workforce expansion, etc., which might affect your employees?

___ 7. Does upper management occasionally run the draft of a new procedure or policy by you for your comments and advice before they finalize it?

___ 8. When you warn upper management about the effects of some policy, procedure, or condition on the workforce, do they give your inputs due consideration?

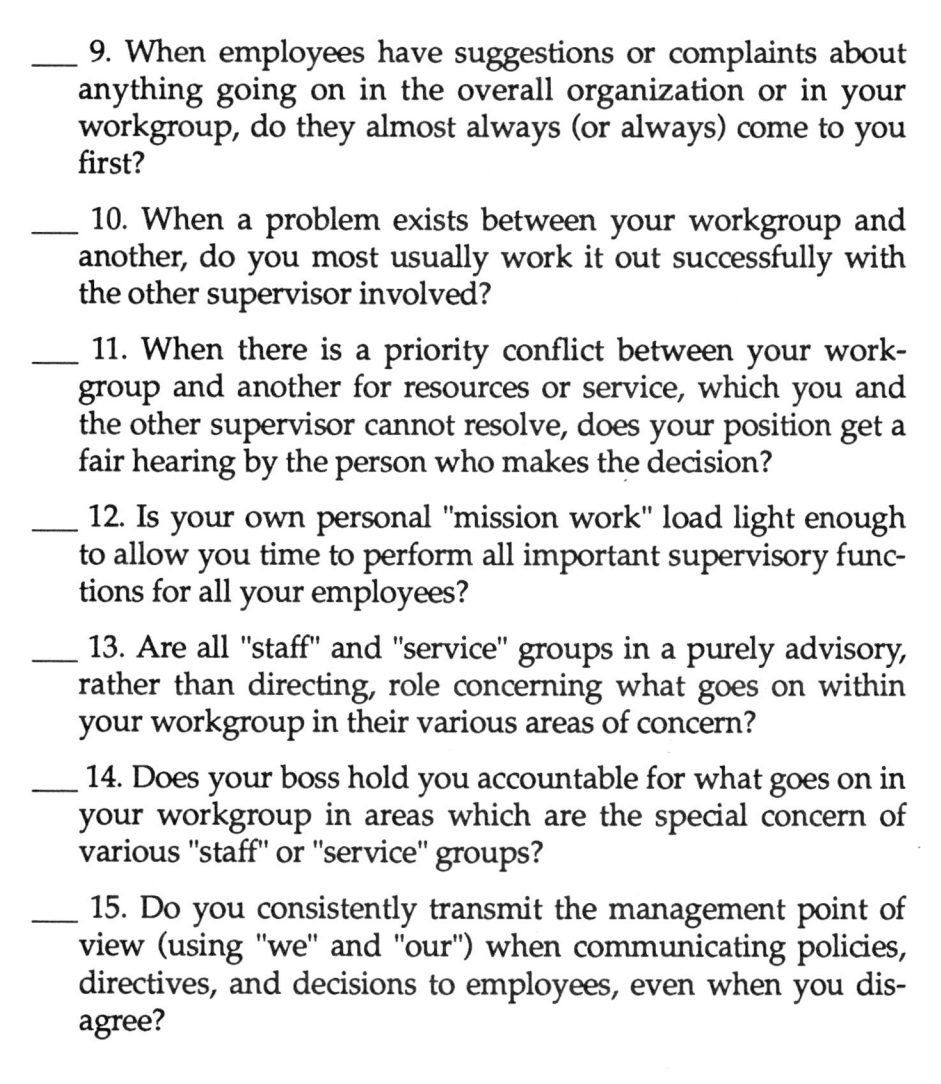

___ 9. When employees have suggestions or complaints about anything going on in the overall organization or in your workgroup, do they almost always (or always) come to you first?

___ 10. When a problem exists between your workgroup and another, do you most usually work it out successfully with the other supervisor involved?

___ 11. When there is a priority conflict between your workgroup and another for resources or service, which you and the other supervisor cannot resolve, does your position get a fair hearing by the person who makes the decision?

___ 12. Is your own personal "mission work" load light enough to allow you time to perform all important supervisory functions for all your employees?

___ 13. Are all "staff" and "service" groups in a purely advisory, rather than directing, role concerning what goes on within your workgroup in their various areas of concern?

___ 14. Does your boss hold you accountable for what goes on in your workgroup in areas which are the special concern of various "staff" or "service" groups?

___ 15. Do you consistently transmit the management point of view (using "we" and "our") when communicating policies, directives, and decisions to employees, even when you disagree?

If you have more than three items left blank, you seriously need to talk to your boss about your supervisory role.

Exercises

Exercise One

When is it Reasonable to Expect Your Boss to Back You Up?

Mark each item either:

"A"= Manager should let Supervisor's decision stand as-is.

"B"= Manager should let Supervisor's decision stand just this once, but caution the Supervisor on more appropriate action to take in the future.

"C"= Manager should reverse the decision.

"D"= Manager should ask the Supervisor to reverse it.

___ 1. You assign a worker some continuing duties which are outside the worker's classification. Worker (and steward) complain to manager.

___ 2. Safety specialist recommends you hold up operation until broken glass and splintered lumber can be cleared from the work area. Because of heavy schedule pressures, you decide to operate anyway, and inform workers of the hazard and instruct them on how to avoid it. The Safety Supervisor complains to the manager that you are running a high accident risk, and wants the operation shut down.

___ 3. You reprimand a worker for negligence and insubordination. Worker files a grievance. Manager, in the appropriate stage of the grievance procedure, discovers you had not given clear instruction for the worker to follow, and worker was not at fault.

___ 4. You submit an employee for a $200.00 a month salary increase. This gets cut to $100.00 during the review and approval process. However, through a clerical error in the wage and salary department, you get notified the $200.00 increase has been approved. You tell the employee he/she will get a $200.00 raise. The paycheck, however, comes with only $100.00 increase. The employee complains to you and you appeal to upper management to back your promise to the employee.

___ 5. You're fed up with an employee, so you recommend discharge and tell the employee to expect termination in about two weeks. Manager reviews the case and finds no documentation of warnings, reprimands, plans for improvement, or target dates and objectives.

___ 6. You recommend discharge of a worker for repeated infractions about which the employee had been warned. Although discharge is allowed for this offense, Union contends it is too harsh a punishment. Industrial relations reviews the case and finds you within your rights. However, they suggest to your manager that if we can concede this one, the Union has agreed to drop a work-rule arbitration which looks as if it will cost the organization thousands of dollars.

___ 7. On Friday you approve personal time off for all employees to attend an ex-employee's wedding from 2:00 to 4:30 p.m. Tuesday. Tuesday morning, your manager discovers this and realizes your department will be closed to customers and other workgroups for the late afternoon.

Answers to Exercise One

When is it reasonable to expect your boss to back you up?

Mark each item either:

"A"= Manager should let the Supervisor's decision stand as-is.

"B"= Manager should let the Supervisor's decision stand just this once, but caution the Supervisor on more appropriate action to take in the future.

"C"= Manager should reverse the decision.

"D"= Manager should ask the Supervisor to reverse it.

_D_ 1. You assign a worker some continuing duties which are outside the worker's classification. Worker (and steward) complain to manager.

_B_ 2. Safety specialist recommends you hold up operation until broken glass and splintered lumber can be cleared from the work area. Because of heavy schedule pressures, you decide to operate anyway, and inform workers of the hazard and instruct them on how to avoid it. The safety supervisor complains to the manager that you are running a high accident risk and wants the operation shut down.

_D_ 3. You reprimand a worker for negligence and insubordination. Worker files a grievance. Manager, in the appropriate stage of the grievance procedure, discovers you had not given clear instruction for the worker to follow, and worker was not at fault.

_A_ 4. You submit an employee for a $200 a month salary increase. This gets cut to $100 during the review and approval process. However, through a clerical error in the wage and salary department, you get notified the $200 increase has been approved. You tell the employee he/she will get a $200 raise. The paycheck, however, comes with only $100 increase. The employee complains to you and you appeal to upper management to back your promise to the employee.

_D_ 5. You're fed up with an employee, so you recommend discharge and tell the employee to expect termination in about two weeks. Manager reviews the case, and finds no documentation of warnings, reprimands, plans for improvement, or target dates and objectives.

_D_ 6. You recommend discharge of a worker for repeated infractions about which the employee had been warned. Although discharge is allowed for this offense, union contends it is too harsh a punishment. Industrial relations reviews the case, and finds you within your rights. However, they suggest to your manager that if we can concede this one, the union has agreed to drop a work-rule arbitration which looks as if it will cost the organization thousands of dollars.

_B_ 7. On Friday you approve personal time off for all employees to attend an ex-employee's wedding from 2:00 to 4:30 p.m. Tuesday. Tuesday morning your manager discovers this and realizes your department will be closed to customers and other workgroups for the late afternoon!

Exercise Two

Back 'em up?

There recently has been a big push on security in your building, and one issue that has been emphasized is that employees should challenge any unescorted visitors they see wandering about.

Yesterday, one of your people sees a stranger, unescorted and obviously bewildered. She turns out to be the buyer's representative from one of your major customers, looking for the Works Manager's office. Not wanting to risk alienating an important person like this, your employee decides to escort her personally to the Works Manager's office since you were not around.

Your employee felt that holding the buyer's representative until a security guard arrived would surely be seen as inhospitable, and just directing her to the Works Manager's office would still leave an unauthorized person walking around unescorted.

However, this took your employee away from his/her workstation without permission, a clear violation of work rules. While he/she was gone, the General Manager called for some important information and got no answer!

The first you hear about all this is when the General Manager calls to tell you the employee is negligent and asks you to reprimand him/her.

Questions (for Exercise Two):

1. What's the first thing you would do?
(Check one only)

    ___ A. Tell the General Manager to go to h---!

    ___ B. Reprimand the employee as directed by the G.M.

    ___ C. Check with the employee to see what happened.

    ___ D. Ask the G.M. to do it himself/herself.

2. Would you then issue the reprimand? ___ Yes ___ No

3. If you do not issue the reprimand, what would you do?
(Check one only)

    ___ A. Tell the employee he did the right thing, and should do likewise on any similar situations in the future.

    ___ B. Tell the employee you'll stand behind him/her, but to choose a different action next time.

    ___ C. Tell the employee he/she has a problem with the G.M. and suggest they go talk to the G.M. to straighten it out.

    ___ D. Tell the employee you think he/she did the right thing, but you have to file a reprimand just to keep the G.M. happy.

4. What would be your stand with the G.M.?
(Check all that apply)

    ___ A. Explain the circumstances. Point out that even if the employee violated a rule, he/she did so with the best interest of the organization at heart. Even if he/she made a wrong judgement, he/she should not be reprimanded.

    ___ B. Defend the employee's judgement as the only thing which could have been done. Argue with the G.M. to show him any other courses of action he feels the employee could have taken are ridiculous.

___ C. Admit that some of the blame is probably yours for not emphasizing enough the rule about leaving a workstation without permission. Suggest that employee should not be reprimanded for your error.

___ D. To get the G.M. off his demand for a reprimand, point out his stupidity for commanding a reprimand before he even had the facts.

5. Suppose the G.M. insists? What do you do then?

(Check one only)

___ A. Resign

___ B. Tell the G.M. he'll have to do it himself, because you refuse.

___ C. Issue the reprimand

___ D. Take the case to the G.M.'S boss (the Works Manager).

6. Will the actions you've chosen cause employees to see you as a member-of-management who looks out for their interests?

___ Yes ___ No

Answers to Exercise Two

Back 'em up?

There recently has been a big push on security in your building, and one issue that has been emphasized is that employees should challenge any unescorted visitors they see wandering about.

Yesterday, one of your people sees a stranger, unescorted and obviously bewildered. She turns out to be the buyer-representative from one of your major customers, looking for the Works Manager's office. Not wanting to risk alienating an important person like this, your employee decides to escort her personally to the Works Manager's office since you were not around.

Your employee felt that holding the buyer-representative until a security guard arrived would surely be seen as inhospitable, and just directing her to the Works Manager's office would still leave an unauthorized person walking around unescorted.

However, this took your employee away from his/her workstation without permission, a clear violation of work rules. While he/she was gone, the General Manager called for some important information and got no answer.

The first you hear about all this is when the General Manager calls to tell you the employee is negligent and asks you to reprimand him/her.

1. What's the first thing you would do?

(Check one only)

    ___ A. Tell the General Manager to go to h---!

    ___ B. Reprimand the employee as directed by the G.M.

    _X_ C. Check with the employee to see what happened.

    ___ D. Tell the G.M. to do it himself.

2. Would you then issue the reprimand? _?_ Yes _?_ No

3. If you do not issue the reprimand, what would you do?
(Check one only)

    ___ A. Tell the employee he/she did the right thing and should do likewise in any similar situations in the future.

    _X_ B. Tell the employee you'll stand behind him/her but next time to choose a different action.

    ___ C. Tell the employee he/she has a problem with the G.M. and suggest they go talk to the G.M. to straighten it out.

    ___ D. Tell the employee you think he/she did the right thing, but you have to file a reprimand just to keep the G.M. happy.

4. What would be your stand with the G.M.?

(Check all that apply)

    _X_ A. Explain the circumstances. Point out that even if the employee violated a rule, he/she did so with the best interest of the organization at heart. Even if he/she made a wrong judgement, he/she should not be reprimanded.

    ___ B. Defend the employee's judgement as the only thing which could have been done. Argue with the G.M. to show him any other courses of action he feels the employee could have taken are ridiculous.

    _X_ C. Admit that some of the blame is probably yours for not emphasizing enough the rule about leaving a workstation without permission. Suggest that employee should not be reprimanded for your error.

    ___ D. To get the G.M. off his demand for a reprimand, point out his stupidity for commanding a reprimand before he even had the facts.

5. Suppose the G.M. insists? What do you do then?

(Check one only)

___ A. Resign
___ B. Tell the G.M. he'll have to do it himself, because you refuse.
_X_ C. Issue the reprimand
___ D. Take the case to the G.M.'s boss (the Works Manager)

(There is no best answer if the issue goes this far.)

Exercise Three

No Wonder

Howie Dune, inspection supervisor, complains that his bosses never include him in planning discussions for procedures or policies that will affect his workgroup. "In addition," Howie says, "Even when I make a recommendation to improve output, they don't listen. Three months ago, I got together with a couple of my inspectors, and we figured out a way to get more parts through the inspection line while, at the same time, making the inspectors 'jobs easier. It's a good idea, but it will require a change in the inspection slips and a reorganization of one job in the production department. So, I wrote it up and sent it in to management. But as usual, I haven't heard a thing back. They'll probably bury it like they do every other thing I send in."

"They say they want you to recommend improvements, but when you do, they never act on them. Just look at the ideas I've laid on my boss to make the inspector's lot in life easier:

* A 15-minute eye-rest break every hour to ease eye strain from detailed scrutiny of finished pieces.

* Air-conditioned cushions on the work stools. Cool seat, cool head, I always say.

* Free coffee, tea, soft drinks, and rolls to show inspectors that the company doesn't consider them as second-class citizens after all.

* Job enrichment, by letting each inspector set his/her own working hours, work schedules, and output quotas."

"Every chance I get, I hammer at the boss to provide more benefits to the workers, but every idea gets lost or turned down."

Questions
(for Exercise Three):

1. Whose team does upper management probably see Howie on?

2. Which of the reasons for lack of managerial confidence does Howie display?

(Check all that apply)

___ A. Identifies with worker team, not management team

___ B. "Tunnel vision"

___ C. Poor judgement

___ D. Lack of knowledge about the group's work

___ E. Keeping managers uninformed

___ F. Asking managers to make his decision for him

3. Do Howie's workers probably see him as a member-of-management?

___ Yes ___ No

4. Since Howie is obviously ineffective at representing workers to management, how effective do you think he is at representing management to workers?

(Check only one)

___ A. Very effective

___ B. Not very effective

___ C. It doesn't matter; they love him for going to bat for them and will do anything for him.

Answers to Exercise Three

No Wonder

1. Whose team does upper management probably see Howie on?

   Worker team

2. Which of the reasons for lack of managerial confidence does Howie display?

(Check all that apply)

   _X_ A. Identifies with worker team, not management team

   _X_ B. "Tunnel vision"

   _X_ C. Poor judgement

   ___ D. Lack of knowledge about the group's work

   ___ E. Keeping managers uninformed

   ___ F. Asking managers to make his decision for him

3. Do Howie's workers probably see him as a member-of-management?

   ___ Yes _X_ No

4. Since Howie is obviously ineffective at representing workers to management, how effective do you think he is at representing management to workers?

(Check one only)

   ___ A. Very effective

   _X_ B. Not very effective

   ___ C. It doesn't matter, they love him for going to bat for them and will do anything for him.

Recommendation

In order to obtain the best implementation results from reading this book, it is strongly recommended that you discuss the main issues of supervision with your boss.

In order to make that communication easier for you, we have prepared the following memo which you could use to facilitate that discussion and at the same time outline the main issue of this book to your manager.

In the meeting with your manager you should expect to come up with a mutually-agreed-upon area of responsibilities for your supervisory job.

TO: _____ (your manager)

FROM: _____ (you)

SUBJECT: The Organizational Role of Supervisors

DATE: _____

I have just completed PMI's book on the subject of The Organizational Role of Supervisors, which deals with the supervisor as a position on the "management team."

I have listed the main issues covered in the book for your information. I also request that we meet soon and discuss your views on these subjects so that we can come up with mutually agreed upon duties for my job.

* Supervisors have mission workers reporting directly to them.

* Managers have supervisors (or other managers) reporting to them.

* Managers should be more concerned about managing resources so that they will be available when needed for tomorrow rather than worrying about how the work is being done today.

* As a head-of-workgroup, the Supervisor, not the Manager, should be seeing to it that the work comes out with quality, timeliness, accuracy, cost control, safety, etc.

* The job of coordinating a supervisor's unit with a unit headed by another supervisor belongs primarily to the Supervisors.

* In order to be effective, the Supervisor must be seen by workers and managers as a member-of-management.

* There are many duties which this book suggests belong to a supervisor as a head-of-workgroup. (I would like to discuss these duties with you so that we can come up with a few key issues that you want me to work on.)

* Coordinating with other supervisors is the second major role of a supervisor. (In order to perform well under this duty, I need your help in understanding some of the main pressures, problems, and functions of other units with which my unit interacts.

* For a supervisor to be effective, a supervisor must be seen by managers and by mission workers as a member-of-management. This important position can be eroded by managers and other staff functions. (I would like to discuss with you what my views are in this regard.)

Please let me know at your earliest convenience when you can set aside some time to discuss these items. If you wish, I can give you my copy of this book so that you can obtain more detailed information on the summary points I have listed above.